SHE SANG FOR INDIA

*How M.S. Subbulakshmi
Used Her Voice for Change*

Written by **Suma Subramaniam**

Illustrated by **Shreya Gupta**

FARRAR STRAUS GIROUX

New York

T0032691

Kunjamma, *the little one,* lived in a house filled with rhythm and beat. Her grandmother, mother, and sister strummed the violin, tambura, and veena. Her brother's fingers struck plum-jham-nam-dhim-thom on a mridangam.

Kunja sang. So sweet was her tone, so clear was her rising and lowering notes of Sa-Ri-Ga-Ma-Pa-Dha-Ni, that of all the instruments, her favorite was her voice.

But Kunja was not free to sing everywhere. She was a small-town devadasi girl whose voice was meant only to please gods and kings. Girls were not admitted to most public concerts—if they were invited to perform, festivals were canceled, or people walked out in protest.

Why should women be confined by powerful men? Kunja's blossoming voice filled her mother with hope. She wanted her daughter to be known and recognized for her talent. She pulled little Kunja away from playing with mud pies and prodded her to sing a few songs at a school.

Kunja's notes spun and swirled in the air. An audience member reached out to the family to make a gramophone record. Kunja's mother agreed. Her voice became known. The meaning of her full name on the record label was a song of its own.

"Maragatha Vadivum"
Song by Madurai Shanmukhavadivu Subbulakshmi, age 10 years

Madurai, after the city where she was born
Shanmukhavadivu, the echo of her mother's name
Subbulakshmi, the goddess of heavenly wealth

A melodious name for a melodious girl.

As a teenager, Subbulakshmi performed with her
mother at intimate, private gatherings. She learned
Carnatic music from several masters . . .

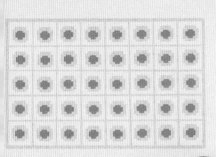

. . . until one day, a letter arrived from the prestigious Madras Music Academy. Subbulakshmi's heart leapt when she opened it. Would she be the first woman invited to sing there?

Her dream faded.

The academy did not want to hear her voice. Instead, she was invited to attend a workshop at their conference. Subbulakshmi was still just an audience member.

But she was eager to learn. She became friends with other women attending the conference. With their encouragement, she traveled to nearby towns by train, bus, and bullock cart. Everywhere, she was the only woman among the singers. And she was never offered the best time slot to perform.

Her path was long, but Subbulakshmi was determined.
After every song, she bowed, and in her smile, the audience
saw a glimmer of her strength.

She sang at several small cultural
and religious festivals until
music lovers couldn't
ignore her voice.

Fewer and fewer people cared about the old ways, which said that girls were not permitted to perform. The audiences roared. Their cheers reached the doors of the Madras Music Academy again, forcing the men to take notice. When Subbulakshmi was sixteen years old, the Madras Music Academy finally broke from tradition and invited her to sing.

With her mother playing the tambura beside her, Subbulakshmi was no longer just an audience member. She was a star—the first woman and the youngest musician to perform at the academy.

But as the years passed, Subbulakshmi's heart became heavy. In the 1940s, India was trying to gain independence from British rule. People were arrested and killed at protests and marches.

Mahatma Gandhi, India's peaceful visionary, invited her to sing at charity concerts all over the country.

At first, thirty-one-year-old Subbulakshmi hesitated. She worried that her music would not be meaningful enough for her people. But if she didn't use her voice for freedom, what use was she?

वन्दे मातरम्
vande mataram

Salutations to you, Mother India

Freedom came with a heavy price. British India was divided into two countries—India and Pakistan. Subbulakshmi thought about the millions of neighbors and friends forced to flee their homes amid bloodshed.

She took a deep breath and sang:

ஒளிபடைத்த கண்ணினாய் வா வா வா

oli padaitha kaNNinaai vaa vaa vaa

The one whose eyes are filled with light—come, come, come.

Four months later, Gandhi was assassinated. Subbulakshmi's entire country was drowning in sorrow. She could bear the grief no more. She sang through her tears. She sang to heal. Her voice was heard on every radio station in the country.

हरि तुम हरो जन की पीर

hari tum haro jana kī pīr

*Hari, take away the
sufferings of your slaves.*

Subbulakshmi was invited to sing at the United Nations.
She was the first Indian musician ever asked to perform there.
This was her chance—to share her music, to show her strength,
to offer her country peace.

The day before the concert, Subbulakshmi's throat turned sore.
She could barely talk. And then she lost her voice.

But she would not give up. Subbulakshmi was determined to sing
for herself, her gurus, her family, her friends, her fans back home,
and for the world.

When showtime arrived, she sat on the stage, cross-legged, and leaned toward the microphone. She listened to the rhythm of the tambura. She hummed until her face relaxed. Notes fluttered out from her mouth. Words curled from her lips. She regained the chirp of her voice!

Madurai Shanmukhavadivu Subbulakshmi was a woman, an activist, and a musician. So she did her best to bring change and to offer hope.

She sang.

मैत्रीं भजत अखिलहृज्जेत्रीम्

आत्मवदेव परानपि पश्यत ।

युद्धं त्यजत स्पर्धां त्यजत

त्यजत परेषु अक्रमम् आक्रमणम् ॥

जननी पृथिवी कामदुघाऽऽस्ते

जनको देवः सकलदयालुः ।

दाम्यत दत्त दयध्वं जनताः

श्रेयो भूयात् सकलजनानाम् ॥

maitrīṃ bhajata akhilahṛjjetrīm

ātmavadeva parānapi paśyata |

yuddhaṃ tyajata spardhāṃ tyajata

tyajata pareṣu akramam ākramaṇam ||

jananī pṛthivī kāmadughā(ā)ste

janako devaḥ sakaladayāluḥ |

dāmyata datta dayadhvaṃ janatāḥ

śreyo bhūyāt sakalajanānām ||

Let us develop friendship and look upon others as
    ourselves.

Let us abandon our differences, hate, and rivalry.

Let us develop compassion and respect the earth
    as our mother.

Let all of humanity come together for peace.

Dear Reader,

M.S. Subbulakshmi's life is an example of how a small-town girl with a great devotion to her craft realized her dream. In her time, it was rare for a woman to make a mark in the world. I wrote this story because through this astounding human being's life, we can learn that the ability to heal ourselves and the world is within us.

Subbulakshmi lived simply throughout the 1900s. She had no yearning for fancy things, clothes, or jewelry. Her humility and love for Carnatic music was the lifeline of her soul, and she followed it. It led her to people and places she'd never imagined. A few of those people cared deeply about her success and helped pave the way for her growth. She even acted in films.

Soon, fans strove to be like her. They dressed like her, with the round red vermillion on her forehead, her popular hand-woven sari in blue, and a circle of jasmine flowers in her hair. In her husband, T. Sadasivam, Subbulakshmi found a friend and a guide. With him by her side, she rose to fame.

But Subbulakshmi's life was not always full of joys. She suffered financial difficulties and many ailments. She pushed through these struggles with hard work, enthusiasm, and dedication to singing. She became the main source of economic support for her family. She learned and sang in many languages. This story has references to her songs in Tamil, Hindi, and Sanskrit.

Her music career lasted for more than seven decades, and she gave away most of what she earned to charity. She was the first musician to receive the Bharat Ratna—India's highest civilian honor. She was also the first Indian musician to receive the Ramon Magsaysay Award, considered the Nobel Prize of Asia, for her contribution to public service through her music.

Subbulakshmi continues to live through her songs. Her rendition of "Sri Venkateshwara Suprabhatam" is played every morning in temples and in the homes of millions of Indians across the globe, including mine. With Subbulakshmi's story and songs in your heart, I hope you are inspired to find your own power and voice.

Sincerely,

Suma Subramaniam

MORE ABOUT CARNATIC MUSIC

Carnatic music is an ancient system of classical music popular in South India. It is performed by an ensemble of musicians consisting of a singer or singers, a violinist, a person playing a tambura, and a rhythmic accompaniment. The music concert can take place in a temple, welcoming the public, or in a large auditorium.

GLOSSARY

Carnatic (kar-naa-tick): a system of classical music popular in the southern part of India. This form of music began in the fifteenth century. It is associated with Hinduism, a major religion in India.

mridangam (mri-dun-gum): a barrel-shaped, double-headed drum.

sari (sa-ree): a long piece of fabric that many Indian women wear draped around their bodies. A sari is usually worn with a blouse and a skirt.

tambura (tham-boo-rah): a large, four-stringed lute that produces a steady sound and accompanies singing or other musical instruments.

veena (vee-nah): a plucked string instrument with a lute-like body and a gourd fitted at each end to serve as resonators.

M.S. SUBBULAKSHMI'S TIMELINE

- September 16, 1916: Madurai Shanmukhavadivu Subbulakshmi is born in Madurai, India.
- 1926: Subbulakshmi's first recording is released when she is ten years old.
- 1929: Subbulakshmi gives her first performance at the prestigious Madras Music Academy, which breaks tradition by opening the doors to a young, female devadasi singer.
- 1936: Subbulakshmi meets T. "Kalki" Sadasivam, a freedom fighter, singer, journalist, and film producer.

- 1938: Subbulakshmi's first feature film, *Sevasadanam*, dealing with women's rights, is released.
- 1940: Subbulakshmi marries Sadasivam.
- 1947: India gains independence.
- 1963: Subbulakshmi performs for the first time at the Edinburgh International Festival of Music and Drama.
- 1966: Subbulakshmi performs at the UN General Assembly in Carnegie Hall, New York.
- 1968: Subbulakshmi becomes the first woman to receive the title of Sangita Kalanidhi from the Madras Music Academy.
- 1974: Subbulakshmi becomes the first Indian musician to receive the Ramon Magsaysay Award (considered Asia's Nobel Prize).
- 1982: Subbulakshmi performs at the Royal Albert Hall in London.
- 1987: Subbulakshmi performs at the Festival of India in Moscow.
- 1997: Subbulakshmi's husband, Sadasivam, passes away.
- 1998: Subbulakshmi becomes the first musician to receive the Bharat Ratna, the highest civilian honor of the Republic of India.
- December 11, 2004: Subbulakshmi passes away.
- October 2016: The UN releases a postage stamp to honor the legacy of M.S. Subbulakshmi and to mark fifty years since she performed at the General Assembly.

SELECTED BIBLIOGRAPHY

*Many thanks to Smt. S. Aishwarya, the great-granddaughter of M.S. Subbulakshmi,
for sharing personal stories and pictures.*

Advaita Vedanta. "M S Subbulakshmi Live Performance at UN Concert on 23rd Oct. 1966." January 10, 2014. YouTube video, 9:19. https://www.youtube.com/watch?v=ArOsyp6dSLE.

T. J. S. George. *MS: A Life in Music*. New Delhi: HarperCollins Publishers India, 2007.

Gowri Ramnarayan. *MS & Radha: Saga of Steadfast Devotion*. Chennai: Wordcraft, 2008.

Lakshmi Viswanathan. *Kunjamma: Ode to a Nightingale*. New Delhi: Lustre Press, 2003.

To my family, who shared their love
for Carnatic music with me.

And to S. Aishwarya and S. Saundarya,
who keep their great-grandmother's legacy alive.

And to the fans of M.S. Subbulakshmi everywhere in the world.

—S. S.

To my wonderful mentor Andrea Spooner for
her guidance, support, and encouragement.

—S. G.

Farrar Straus Giroux Books for Young Readers
An imprint of Macmillan Publishing Group, LLC
120 Broadway, New York, NY 10271 • mackids.com

Text copyright © 2022 by Suma Subramaniam.
Illustrations copyright © 2022 by Shreya Gupta.
All rights reserved.

Our books may be purchased in bulk for promotional, educational, or business use. Please
contact your local bookseller or the Macmillan Corporate and Premium Sales Department at
(800) 221-7945 ext. 5442 or by email at MacmillanSpecialMarkets@macmillan.com.

Library of Congress Cataloging-in-Publication Data is available.

First edition, 2022
Color separations by Embassy Graphics
Printed in China by RR Donnelley Asia Printing Solutions Ltd.,
Dongguan City, Guangdong Province

ISBN 978-0-374-38874-4 (hardcover)
1 3 5 7 9 10 8 6 4 2

The text in this book was set in Wilke Lt Std and the display type was set in Restora.
Art directed and designed by Sharismar Rodriguez and Neil Swaab.

Production was supervised by John Nora, and the production editors were Ilana Worrell
and Jacqueline Hornberger. Edited by Elizabeth Lee and Trisha de Guzman.